Selina Nwulu is a Yorkshire-b[...] [...]rian heritage. Based in London, she is a w[...] [...]es her work to explore global polit[...] [...]ging, all of which she sprink[...]

She has perforn[...] [...]nternationally including at Glas[...] [...]nbank Centre, mac birmingham, the [...] [...]entre, the Albany, and Ruigoord Festival in [...]

Her poetry has been published in a number of anthologies and she has also written articles for the Free Word Centre, *Red Pepper*, the *Guardian*, and Africa Writes.

The Secrets I Let Slip

Selina Nwulu

Burning Eye

Copyright © 2015 Selina Nwulu

The author asserts the moral right under the Copyright, Designs and Patents Act 1988 to be identified as the author of this work.

All rights reserved. No part of this publication may be reproduced, stored in a retrieval system, or transmitted, in any form or by any means without the prior written consent of the author, nor be otherwise circulated in any form of binding or cover other than that in which it is published and without a similar condition being imposed on the subsequent purchaser.

This edition published by Burning Eye Books 2015

www.burningeye.co.uk
@burningeyebooks

Burning Eye Books
15 West Hill, Portishead, BS20 6LG

ISBN 978 1 90913 649 6

Contents

Our Parents' Children	7
Tough Dragons	8
Curriculum Vitae	9
Encyclopaedia	11
Two Sides of a Coin	12
There Is a Woman Wailing on the 118 to Brixton	13
Foreign	14
Friends, You Are Ageing Beautifully	15
Be Silent	16
Homecoming – Pt I	17
Fluid Prejudice	19
Kettled	20
Betrayal	21
Before	22
Rotherham, I Remember	23
Jack in a Box	24
Flamethrowers	25
Closing	26
Too Many	27
Hollow	28
Cuppa	29
Catastrophe	30
Common Language	31
Homecoming – Pt II	32
Wild Grass	33
Acknowledgements	34

Our Parents' Children

*All immigrants are artists – re-creating your entire life is a form of
reinvention on par with the greatest works of literature.*
                                                    Edwidge Danticat

Theirs was the first gamble.
Hopes stitched into suitcase linings
before being searched at customs.

An airport poster:
We cannot assume responsibility for lost belongings.

Many will not speak of what was lost and found.
How tectonic plates shift the roots of home,
how their cracks give birth to:

border control
the smack of periphery
a dangerous refuge.

They will not speak of this,
of the daily artistry needed to survive,
of how home is hard to grow
on barren ground.

But we carry this journey through our veins.
Their footsteps are woven into our birthmarks;
their struggles, the skin under our nails.
This is our inheritance,
passed down like guilt heirlooms
we carry this through to
the other side of reinvention.

They will not speak of this,
yet we know these truths through
the cracks on the ground we try not to walk on.

They will put their hopes into our hands,
the pain is in letting them go.

Tough Dragons

She draws the cliffs of Llanberis and sends it to
the only person who would cry and understand.

It's morning and she can still feel the day in her hands.
The morning she stood up to her father,

she trembled, wearing a scarf from Morocco:
This place is my bones; I don't care if you don't like it.

He said:
You are fiercely intelligent and when you figure out how to use them, your words will slay the toughest of dragons.

She clears her wardrobe, giving away clothes she doesn't recognise herself in.

Curriculum Vitae

One summer I dreamt in French for the first time.
I backpacked, got stranded in Prague, slept by French lakes
and fell in whimsy with inappropriate boys (from afar).

Later, I would escape to a dot in the Indian Ocean.
I'd rediscover my skin in rich mahogany,
sleep on mountain tops and never see so many stars.
For a second I would taste freedom.

You travelled where?
sneers the First Suit, headbutting my thoughts.
OK, sure, fine – but what did you actually do?

Bird song memories morph into the shrill
of job centre phones. The Suit's eyebrows
nail me to the chair. The wind disappears,
caution re-finds me and sits on my shoulder,
regrets hiss at my ear –
another stagnant statistic becoming.

Weeks roll on, to-and-fro, to-and-fro.
Signed on. Switched off. Monotonous actions
in the room of tripped ambition. And I do learn
new tricks, like finding strength in my words
and learning how to make the perfect cup of
green tea during the commercial breaks of
Come Dine with Me.

Daytime re-runs, time passes and my life
becomes a klaxon, the job centre pulls
on my reins and squeezes my mind of its optimism.

So what kind of employment are you looking for?
parrots Suit Two.

I want to write. I want to save myself
and the world from its suffocating anguish.
I want to give a damn, honestly I do, because

in a world that turns in lust for
yen, dollar, sterling, I want to do something more,
something that really matters.
Do you know what I mean?

So… communications, then?

Suit Two misspells *communication*.
I sink further in my polyester seat,
look skyward but can't see the stars
anymore, just the plaster ceiling cracks.

So what exactly are you doing to look for work?
sighs Suit Three.

I'm falling in love with jobs that pay me back
in silence and automated emails.

I'm having my heart broken by rejection messages,
informing me of unsuccessful applications.

I'm trying to woo and charm recruiters but in a crowd
of desperate people I'm just another pixel in a billboard poster.

I used to think I was somebody.
But sitting in this doleful room,
I watch all of my armour,
these adventures and life philosophies,
tumble around my feet.

Till I am left, whittled down to a crisp CV
polluted with half plans and exaggerations.

I speak several languages, you know.
I can very nearly juggle with four balls.
I did a course in French sign language.
My grandmother lived till she was 108.
I once hiked a volcano.
I make a mean chickpea stew.

I don't think you care.

Encyclopaedia

He thinks me an encyclopaedia,
scrapes his fingers through the depths of my chapters
and tries to rip my binding
so he can separate and hang up my pages,
searching for proof of my sadness.
He will not stop until every line has been conquered,
will not rest till all words have been crushed into their vowels.

He thinks me an encyclopaedia
and then wonders why I have become a closed book.

Two Sides of a Coin

There is a girl, who looks like me,
walking through the streets of Lagos.
She is freshly plucked mangoes and forehead beads of sweat.
She is flat shoes and a head wrap on Sundays.
She is a collision of patterns chasing each other.

She looks like me but her vowel sounds have shrunk,
there are no Yorkshire undertones here.
Instead she speaks in half songs,
rolls Igbo off her tongue like blooming hibiscus
and wears her ancestors' sayings on her chest like armour.

She weaves through this downtown scene in fluid choreography:
the joke thrown to a passing neighbour,
the pause and smell of the pile of peppers in the market.
Each act has a home in this moving composition,
you can see her belonging in the sway of her hips.

If you look closely enough,
you can see how her shoulders sigh like mine,
can hear her life in the drag of her flat feet
and feel their tendency to wander.
We both laugh with the weight and depth of a church bell.
On a good day it will throw our heads back.

Sometimes I see these two versions of myself
like two sides of a coin: heads – here, tails – over there.
I wonder why the coin landed on this side.
I wonder which version would have laughed the most.

There is a Woman Wailing on the 118 to Brixton

She is sighing a new song
shaking her head and
rocking herself like a reverse lullaby
Son dead oh
whispered to the bus ceiling
each word a piece of shrapnel
her grief a force field
Son dead oh
the 118 jerks us to where
we are going
or leaving
and we sit there
in heavy silence
waiting.

Foreign

We are becoming foreign languages to one another
and the joy you get from kissing me is fading.
So when your lips make out shapes
that say *it's not working*
I watch the life we would have had
lose itself like sand in an egg timer.

Friends, You Are Ageing Beautifully

Even your new shades of surrender have their poetry
and yet it seems I am ageing without much conviction.
I feel like I should have at least received some kind of explanation
perhaps in memo or song.

The first wrinkle has appeared – it looks like a snail has lurched
across my forehead and left a trail of its slime.
I'm trying to exude a sage grace and be someone who
rinses their words in philosophy and who is OK with wrinkles.

I am not OK with wrinkles.

Friends, I am growing up without much responsibility.
I thought I would be someone by now, perhaps a rock star.
But while *mortgages, children* and *commitment*
are now blooming taste buds on your tongues,

I still don't own an iron. I drink wine from mugs
and I don't know which grape it came from.
I come home earlier and earlier for no good reason
except the sandwich at the back of the fridge.

Friends, this is a strange new dance.
I fear I am still stuck at the back of the disco doing the moonwalk
and you are all ageing beautifully;
don't leave me behind.

Be Silent

As Egypt shook, I checked the mirror for love handles,
flicked through its featured howls in a magazine,
fists punching through pixels
framed through coffee mug smears.

Newspapers gave me pictures of Palestine
folding in on itself, fleeing from love lost.
Crumpled civilians dodged my doodles
and idle to-do lists.

As my remote switched on Syria,
I checked my stomach in the TV's reflection,
sucked in cheek bones and imagined myself downsized,
the glare of machine guns in the background.

The world spins off its axis.
I misunderstand as I over-tweeze.
I hear my heart beat louder than theirs
until I forget even having remembered.

Homecoming – Pt I

'Go back to where you came from.'

We're going home, she says,
and I think *at last.*
I'm tired of this town,
its stares never got used to me
and this place feels like a cold scowl.

A plane hauls me from the monochrome
and drops me into a whirlpool of Nigerian colour.
I am hit by its everything:
airport lines of waiting,
haggles, rhythms and smells.

The heat wraps its legs around me,
pees in the small of my back.
I stick to the seat of the car
before it throws me up and down,
a yo-yo over potholes.

The village (my village?)
waits for me with arms like palm trees;
they are waving for my homecoming.

The language (my language?)
speaks in songs woven with
echoes and blood ties.
I am out of tune,
its meanings ducking out of my hands.

I am the mosquito's new fruit,
a different taste in a familiar shape.
They suck from me the authenticity
my words cannot give.
I am raw bitten and grateful.

Can I have this?
Can I make this place my own?

I say hello in Igbo to a face I should recognise,
she cackles at my attempts.

I have fallen between the gaps.
I mourn this abyss between two hands
and smell the red clay soil in the cracks of my palms.
Welcome home, darling.

Fluid Prejudice

The very ink with which history is written is merely fluid prejudice.
                                                            Mark Twain

History will not write us well on this day. Will not recall how democracy crowd surfed on our fingertips, the way it fell to our feet once the tear gas came. History will not say how for a second the tear gas looked like fireworks, fierce light duels erupting in our honour, will not have seen when choke and strangle came, will not notice the scowl of police boots all steeled stomp and scuffed vengeance, will not describe the deceptive smooth edges of a baton, will not tell of their guns, will not remember the fire. Later, the newspapers will forget intention, will flirt with facts, will whisper words like *violence antisocial threat*, will sprinkle in dashes of terror, will leave the rest to the night's shadows, to fearful imagination. Doors will be double locked, eyes averted.

Kettled

And when the boots charged
they forced our chants into barricades,
waved batons at our heads
and framed us through transparent prison blockades,

till all we could do was pound feet into tarmac
till all we felt were shockwaves blistering through our spines
till all we could see was our reflection smeared into theirs
till all our words were trampled into the ground
till all we could do was scratch skin into raw disbelief

till there was no one left to fight but each other.

We are a mere collection of atoms shredding and dividing,
we'll be your hooligans before you know it.

Betrayal

Loving and grieving two people at the same time,
feels like I'm cheating on both.

Before

Before

Before illegal
Before becoming the influx, the scar, the stain
Before finding my new name in a scuffed English novel
Before Jane
Before mastering the sturdy handshake
Before never using it
Before swallowing the lilts of my own tongue
Before forcing my mouth to e-nun-ci-ate
Before being misunderstood
Before dreaming of my mother's songs
Before learning the spirals of British decorum
Before *cup of tea, anyone?*
Before yearning for a belonging I could name

Before the sound of my laugh began to decay
Before the grope of polyester
Before my prayers mocked me
Before *Go Home* ricocheted from mouths to vans
Before dreaming of going home
Before each footstep became an apology
Before *how destitute exactly?*
Before *not destitute enough*
Before application refused
Before temporary
Before knowing
Before the stain, the scar, the influx
Before illegal

Before

Rotherham, I Remember

for Maz

Rotherham, you are my father's fear. You are fallen H's and sausage roll grease smeared onto school uniforms. You are postcard-worthy Whiston Meadows and the Canklow council estates myths told me to run from. Rotherham, you are the books I escaped to; the words and lines that wrapped themselves around my imagination and made themselves friends. Rotherham, you are the red bricks I scraped my knuckles against, you are screams unheard, rooms too small, plans forgotten. Rotherham, you are the teen fusion of Yorkshire mix sweets and Mum's jollof rice. You are the bus stop me and Kerry ran to for shelter, scared from learning our new Year 8 fact: acid rain. Rotherham, you are that rain, the rain that traps and corrodes, makes rust out of all of us. Rotherham, you are the monotony that would divide me and Kerry, re-label us acquaintances with only the weather to talk about. Rotherham, you are growing pains; hushed teenage love tales punctuated with bad grammar and vending machine sugar highs. Rotherham, you are school benches, the belly-deep laughter, mixed with the tears and dreams I told Maz about. Rotherham, you are my difference, the stares and classroom whispers that would isolate and cast me as other. Rotherham, you were the ground to my first step, step to my becoming, you are home to scattered reference points within my words, you are mine. So, Rotherham, though I am not ashamed of you, I am not proud. And I won't hide how alien you are to me now, as strange as Yorkshire mix sweets and jollof rice; a taste I never got used to.

Jack in a Box

After Simon Armitage

His hair is steel wool
and his eyes are metal marbles
and his stare is a rusty vice
and his nose is a used test tube
and his mouth is a drawbridge
and the gap between his teeth is a cave
and his words are bats escaping
and his tongue is a jungle
and his laugh is marbled meat
and his chin is coconut husk
and his neck is a faded oak tree
and his shoulders are weathered cliff edges
and his chest is a stained glass window
and his lungs are crushed roses
and his breath is a cobweb come winter
and his stomach is knotted rope
and his arms are ripped Bible pages
and his palms are coffee-stained atlases
and his fingers are homeless
and his legs are burning matches
and his feet are train tracks
and his shadow is blunt pencil
and his tears are chloroform
and his doubts are a lighthouse
and his intentions are two-day-old flowers
and his smile is a dusty piano

and his heart is a jack in a box,
it has not yet opened.

Flamethrowers

Flaming Morons: Thugs And Thieves Terrorise Britain's Streets
                                        Daily Express

6 August 2011.

this day is a ripe old wound exploding. you will find no apologies here, just flamethrowers ripping open their chests, showing the way riots beat against their ribcages daily. whispers behind curtain call them feral, don't they just look like deficits? like they are wearing the faces headlines told you about? look at these hooded would-have-beens, listen to the sound of their footsteps punching tarmac. just for a second, look at how they play, this *underclass*, see how the word blossoms poison in your mouth. you will find no apologies here, just fifteen minutes of table turning, pure revolt before faces become flickered siren blue. before the sweep, the noose, bottled water theft, the spin, the spin, the spin, drip-fed clichés, loopholes becoming smaller. still, you will find no apologies here, flamethrowers can't do much damage to property unless its foundations are already burning.

Closing

The city is closing,
the sky's shutters have come down
and the lampposts exhale their benevolent flickers.
It's 3am on a Thursday
and the city is closing
while we skirt the city's pockets
for dim lit corners
secrets from strangers
one more drink
food that will haunt us come morning.
I am worn and
my good sense belongs to yesterday
but FOMO[1] is a curse, you know,
and the city is closing
and when else in this city
can you be both new and old,
lonely without apology,
let the wind throw out your secrets
from behind you like a cape,
hear the scruff of your own footsteps
and not care of their weary intention?

---

[1] Fear of missing out

Too Many

I
She is searching through galaxies
for planets of common conversation.
The only thing she finds is their loneliness,
they wear it like woollen shawls
they are desperate to shrug off.

II
He stares for too long;
he is carrying them through light years,
through first kisses and forevers.
She notes new wrinkles on her hands,
chips varnish off her nails.
She will be his biggest regret.

III
Why does he smell like damp?
It strangles the conversation,
his decay, the noose around
her neck, tightening.

IV
She knows she'd lose herself in this one.
She'd break herself off into pieces
and watch the ghost of her try to love him.
He'd claim not to understand her and
she'd know it's because she'd burnt everything
so he could waft through the embers and start her again.

V
He scans her face,
searching its landmarks for a place to land on:
partner. lover. friend.
He hovers and lands on friend
and she is overladen and sinking.
Too many have been there before.

Hollow

I can understand the importance
of my mother's motherhood.

And I have watched
crowns placed upon
those who have embraced
the revered entrails of maternity,
those who have draped it in
softness and ample bosom.
I understand.

The truth is far too much
beautiful tangle
too much bruise
for the maternal platitudes
we have inherited,
I understand.

But I am yet to hear anything else
I can earn a crown for
and while I have no desire
to be kept up at night,
winded by the weight of sacrifice,
indecision can weigh just as heavy,
can cause just as many sleepless nights.

A mother can become hollow
waiting and waiting
for a second becoming,
watching her daughter running
in the opposite direction
the cycle of motherhood
disintegrating

a triumph
a tragedy

Cuppa

Put the kettle on.
I'm not being funny but he's well fit
no, you don't understand
they're all sinking in the Mediterranean sea
I'm actually speaking objectively here
our borders have become dense and long
it's more an observation really
his face is near symmetrical
and their ships have burst into splints
it's hypnotising
the sea is bloated with people's limbs
it's post attraction really
I'm appreciating him as a work of art
their memories did not make it either
well, of course I wouldn't say no!
they're all sinking in the Mediterranean sea
but that's not the point
anyway, we still going out Friday?
watch how the bubbles float and pop.
Kettle's boiled.

Catastrophe

If I told you how I truly felt:

The earth's inner core would begin to growl,
its lava would hurl volcanic screams.

The plagues of Egypt would return,
we'd wake covered in locusts and frogs and flies.

The sky would brood a sinister grey,
vomiting thunderbolts like falling javelins.

Trees would throw their leaves at you,
their arthritic roots would gnarl in revulsion .

And see how bright the sun shines today?
Well, it would punch you in your face.

But most importantly,
if I told you how I truly felt
the effortless cool of my demeanour
would shatter
leaving me standing there
unarmed

hopeful

So for both of our sakes
it's best that
I love you
in
secret

Common Language

We speak in fluent sadness
we tear it apart at the seams until
our rooms are feathered with sorrow

the tragic ending of an acquaintance
the abusive husband
the sound breaking ribs might make –
crush. crack.
the depressive neighbour
the clink of empty bottles
how puffed our chests would be
if only we'd been loved more.

We inhale these truths
till our throats are coated with tar
till it is smoke floating in our lungs
and it seeps from our pores.

Is it any wonder that
I have become a screaming censer?
That grief billows through my veins
and I am left burning with it?

Homecoming – Pt II

Exiled into each other,
we declare ourselves as found countries.
We map borders in the lines of each other's hands
before migrating to their arms to
map memory on muscle,
trace nations through veins and
find refuge in the creek of their elbow.

Wild Grass

After Lavinia Greenlaw

My love, the red bricks are still here and so is the sense of loneliness. It is strange to think my roots grew here but I ripped them from their beginnings and tried to plant them elsewhere. The corner shop has closed down. The land is cursed and so is its money. It's gone from beautician, clinician, mechanic to corner shop. My love, the air feels like the moment you step out of an aeroplane and my secrets have been scattered around this town in whispers, glances and broken signs. It gives me a pulsing heat from sternum to ribcage. Mrs Darlington has gone. I have no words for Mr Darlington. Which words can conquer cancer? The first man to make my heart bleed rides his bike in circles on my street. His hair is lost and his beauty has aged, we talk about the weather and the merits of a steady saddle without ever looking at each other. My love, the old garden is a green fire. I watched them crush it one day with rubble and patio, but the grass and weeds have fought back, the green defiant and oblivious.

Acknowledgements

Versions of some of these poems have featured in the following publications:

Homesickness and Exile (Emma Press)
Weatherfronts: climate change and the stories we tell (Tipping Point)
West of the Centre (Burning Eye Books)

Thank you to all friends, family and fellow writers who have helped, encouraged and inspired this collection.

Particular thanks to:

Sai Murray for his time and guidance, Platform and the Shake! collective (Jane Trowell, Zena Edwards and Farzana Khan especially), Harry Man and Roger Robinson for their feedback on early drafts, Zofia Walczak, Kyla Manenti, Grace De Morgan, Mariam Hussain (two poems in this collection are yours) and the Malika's Kitchen community.

For Ugochi, Onyinye, Benita and Tema.

For where my poems began.